Caught in Nepal

OTHER BOOKS BY MIKEL DUNHAM

Non-Fiction

Le Gout du Tibet

*Buddha's Warriors: The Story of the CIA-Backed Tibetan
Freedom Fighters, the Chinese Invasion,
and the Ultimate Fall of Tibet*

Samye: A Pilgrimage to the Birthplace of Tibetan Buddhism

Fiction

Casting for Murder

Stilled Life

Caught in Nepal

Tibetan Refugees Photographing
Tibetan Refugees

Mikel Dunham

Vajra Publications
www.vajrabooks.com.np; www.vajrabookshop

Published by
Vajra Publications
Jyatha, Thamel, Kathmandu, Nepal
Tel.: 977-1-4220562, Fax: 977-1-4246536
e-mail: bidur_la@mos.com.np
www.vajrabooks.com.np; www.vajrabookshop.com

Distributed by
Vajra Book Shop
Kathmandu, Nepal

Copyright: Mikel Dunham, 2011

ISBN No. 978-9937-506-65-6

Printed in Nepal

In Memoriam

Venerable Khenchen Palden Sherab Rinpoche

for Margaret

Genesis

Several years ago, I distributed ten digital cameras to young adult Tibetan refugees living in Nepal. Three of them professed basic photographic skills but none of them had owned a camera.

My deal was straightforward. They received free cameras and I received documentation of the Tibetan refugee experience. This book is the result of that collaboration.

It was never my intention to create a political statement. I encouraged the young photographers to focus on their day-to-day lives. "Don't rule out any picture as too boring," I told them. "Take pictures that Western tourists won't be in a position to take." Politics did emerge as one of the themes of their portfolios, however. A shot of a monk waiting at a public telephone booth to call his parents in Tibet, for instance, carried its own subliminal political connotation.

The photographs are documents in their own right, but the sensitivity with which they were shot reveals the compassion inherent in the Tibetan refugee culture: a people with few opportunities struggling to maintain their way of life in a foreign country.

Mikel Dunham

Nepalis and Tibetans: Neighbors for Two Millennia

Nepal's link with Tibet dates back at least two thousand years, back to a time when Nepal's location placed it dead center along the Indo-Tibetan salt route. Cultural exchange went hand in hand with commerce in spite of the almost impenetrable Himalayan massif that separated the two trading partners.

The relationship deepened in 632 AD, when the Tibetan king, Srongtsan Gampo, wedded a Nepali princess by the name of Brikuti. She arrived in Lhasa, Tibet's capital, as a symbol of Nepali-Tibetan cohesion. But it was her devotion to Buddhism that proved to have a far more long-lasting impact. Buddhism had originated in Nepal nearly a thousand years before, when Siddhartha Gautama, the historical Buddha, was born in Lumbini, in southern Nepal.

At the time of Princess Brikuti's marriage, Tibetans were unfamiliar with Buddhism, Bon-pa being the indigenous religion. To the alarm of the royal animistic priests, King Srongtsan Gampo patronized the religion of his new Nepali wife. He even constructed a temple in the center of Lhasa to house Princess Brikuti's collection of Buddhist statuary, brought with her from Nepal. The temple is called the Jokhang. 1400 years later, it remains Tibet's most sacred building.

It took another 125 years before Buddhism replaced Bon-pa as Tibet's prevailing spiritual path. This occurred in 762 AD, when Tibet's warrior-king Trhisong Detsen sent couriers to Nepal to recruit the famous mystical adept, Padmasambhava. It was Padmasambhava who established Samye, the first Buddhist monastery in Tibet, thereby laying the clerical groundwork for what would eventually become the nation's unique theocracy based on a reincarnate rule of Dalai Lamas.

For many centuries, the Nepali-Tibetan connection remained a stable one, until the 1700s, when the relationship began to fray. An acrimonious rift erupted over Tibet's currency, which was minted by the famed Newari silversmiths of the Kathmandu Valley. Over the years, the silversmiths had been debasing the Tibetan coins by adding copper, thus creating a dispute between Tibet's leader, the 8th Dalai Lama, and the three Malla kings, who ruled separate principalities in the Kathmandu Valley.

In 1769, Prithvi Narayan Shah, a great Gurkha warrior chief, defeated the Malla rulers of Kathmandu and consolidated the surrounding principalities of Nepal into one unified nation. As the first king of the Shah Dynasty, Prithvi Narayan sent word to the 8th Dalai Lama, that – from that time forward – the Nepali silversmiths would revert to minting pure silver coins for the Tibetan realm. In return, he ordered Tibet to devalue the currency already in circulation. The Dalai Lama balked, pointing out that devaluation would unfairly discriminate against those who were left holding the copper-tainted coins. A standoff ensued. The longer the issue remained unresolved, the deeper ill feeling grew between both nations.

Open hostility erupted in 1775, when Nepal attempted to expand its eastern border by invading Sikkim, Tibet's ally. The Dalai Lama's army poured into Sikkim to level the playing field.

Finally, in 1788, the king of Nepal used the unsettled coin dispute as an excuse to invade Tibet. The 8th Dalai Lama panicked and sent an urgent plea to China's Manchu Emperor for military backup. The arrival of Chinese troops tipped the scales just in time to thwart Nepal's military advance. A truce was negotiated: In return for the Gurkhas' withdrawal, Tibet agreed to pay a hefty tribute to Nepal. But once the Gurkhas and Chinese troops left Tibetan territory, the Dalai Lama reneged on his promise. Three years passed with no tribute forthcoming.

The Gurkhas invaded Tibet again in 1791, only this time they captured the stronghold of Shighatse, in southern Tibet. There, they appropriated the monastic treasury of Tashilhunpo, a virtual Ft. Knox of art, gems and precious metals.

The Tibetans struck back – again with the help of Manchu troops – and succeeded in driving back the Gurkhas to Nepal. A new truce was signed in 1792. The Gurkhas were forced to return the spoils of Tashilhunpo and to send a handsome tribute to Peking every five years.

From 1792 forward, the Manchus regarded anything that happened in Tibet as China's business. Nepal's invasion of Tibet alerted the emperor to the rising threat of foreign influence that not only included Nepal, but British-controlled India as well, which had uncomfortably good relations with the Gurkha kings.

As for Nepal's foreign policy, never again would it be possible to make a clear distinction between Tibet and China. Tibet was Nepal's ancient Himalayan brother, but China now loomed in the background like an uninvited stepfather.

In the ensuing decades, however – to the relief of Nepal – the Manchu military became entrenched with a series of conflicts in Mainland China. Chinese "authority" in Lhasa became a political affectation and Nepal knew it.

In 1855, Nepal – still stinging from its 1792 defeat –invaded Tibet for the third time in six decades. Nepal's tactical prediction – that the emperor would be unable to provide military assistance – proved correct. Not only was the 11th Dalai Lama forced to pay tribute to Nepal, but he also had to grant, among other penalties, judicial extraterritoriality to Nepalis living in Lhasa.

By the advent of the 20th century, the Manchu Empire was on its last leg. In 1912, the *Koumintang,* a republican revolutionary party led by Sun Yat-sen, delivered the *coup de grace*. The 268-year-old dynasty collapsed. The last emperor abdicated and China became the *Republic of China*.

The Lhasan government made the most of China's domestic instability: The 13th Dalai Lama expelled the remnants of the Manchu army, enabling Tibet to achieve *de facto* independence – a status that Tibet would enjoy (and Nepal would recognize) for the next four decades.

But there was a new force emerging in China: the communist party led by Mao Zedong. A civil war between the Maoists and the *Koumintang* ensued. In 1949, the *Koumintang* capitulated to Taiwan. Mao assumed the mantle of Supreme Leader in Beijing and China became the *People's Republic of China*.

Then, in 1950, Mao turned his gaze to China's western frontier. In October, his army invaded Tibet under the guise of "liberating the masses" from wealthy landowners and the aristocratic clergy who served the Dalai Lama.

But as it turned out, the Tibetans, who, for centuries, had regarded the Dalai Lama as their god-king, saw no need for "liberation". The emergence of organized Tibetan resistance to Mao's People's Liberation Army was only a matter of time.

By the mid 1950s, in eastern Tibet, monasteries were being razed by Chinese air strikes. Monks, nuns and high lamas were tortured, imprisoned and murdered. By 1957, a grassroots resistance army – the *Chushi Gangdruk* – arose and significantly impeded Mao's timeline to subdue and colonize Tibet. (The CIA took note of the situation and began supporting the

Chushi-Gangdruk with covert training, first in Saipan and later in Camp Hale, Colorado.) By 1958, the freedom fighters had spread to central Tibet, with the *Chushi-Gangdruk* in control of most of the region south of Lhasa, all the way to Tibet's border with India and Nepal.

1958: *Chushi-Gangdruk* calvary, south of Lhasa

5

But by March 1959, the massive deployment of Chinese troops into the Lhasan basin had made Tibetan self-governance untenable.

The Dalai Lama fled for his life. A week later, he and his entourage reached safe haven in India. Upon hearing the news of his escape, tens of thousands of Tibetans began an exodus south, determined to be near their spiritual leader.

For Nepal, Mao's colonization of Tibet was at once militarily threatening, economically sobering, (the Chinese takeover undermined Nepal's ancient trade relations with Tibet) and diplomatically confusing. Over the centuries –in spite of periodic armed conflicts – Tibetans and Nepalis had become more than mere neighbors. Especially in the northern Nepali districts, cross-boundary migration and intermarriage had engendered a hybrid culture. In many of the mountainous regions of Nepal, Tibetan was the lingua franca. Nepal's natural instinct was to support Tibet in its darkest hour.

The Rana clan had held the reins of power in Nepal for a hundred years, leaving the Shah kings mere puppets. This changed in 1950, when India supported Nepal's King Tribhuvan's successful ploy to wrest the reins from the Ranas and to reinstate monarchal power.

There was an additional dynamic: For the first time in its history, Nepal had opened its borders to the outside world. (Nepal's sovereignty would not be recognized by the United Nations until 1955.) Striking the correct balance between new international influences was of the utmost importance. In Nepal, the true strength and design of Mao Zedong remained unknown, so the question of how to respond to China's invasion of Tibet boiled down to this: What did Nepal stand to lose if it supported Tibet?

India helped answer Nepal's quandary.

New Delhi's warming relationship with Beijing – a policy shift championed by Prime Minister Jawaharlal Nehru – resulted in Nehru bearing down on Nepal's government to join India's pro-China position. In 1954, India signed a treaty with China that unequivocally recognized

China's sovereignty over Tibet. India coerced Nepal to sign a similar treaty with China a few months later.

***

As was previously mentioned, the Dalai Lama's flight from Tibet resulted in scores of thousands of Tibetans following him into exile. Eventually, the Tibetan exodus would exceed 100,000. Many refugees ended up in India. Many found their way to Nepal. Many died attempting to cross the 19,000-foot mountain passes of the Himalaya. Many others, who survived the horrific trek and made it to the subcontinent, succumbed to diseases and microbes unknown in their native land.

The *Chushi-Gangdruk* fled Tibet as well. First they camped in northern India, wondering what to do next. Most of the men were war-weary and wished only to discover if their loved ones had safely found refuge in India or Nepal. But there was a sizable contingent of fighters – mostly Khampas, Amdoans and Goloks (warriors from eastern Tibet) – who were against attrition. The Khampas had created the *Chushi-Gangdruk* and were by now hardened soldiers, highly trained, at home in high-altitude guerilla warfare and – perhaps most important – felt that they had nothing to gain by returning to civilian life.

In 1960, a top-secret meeting was held in Darjeeling between the Khampa leaders and the head of the CIA Tibetan Task Force. The Khampas indicated their desire to regroup and create a new headquarters in the remote Nepali principality of Mustang. From there, they could dart into Tibet and attack the PLA, then fall back quickly to Mustang before Mao's army could respond. The CIA was inclined to support the *Chushi-Gangdruk* effort because, militarily, Mustang made some sense. Washington had already ruled out the possibility that Nehru would allow the *Chushi-*

Chushi-Gangdruk, Mustang camp, 1960s

Gangdruk to conduct cross-border raids from Indian territory. Mustang, on the other hand, was nominally part of Nepal. It jutted up into the plateau of Tibet and was populated by ethnic Tibetans. The Maharaja of Mustang was Buddhist, so there was no question where his sympathies lay. And finally, the CIA counted on the Nepalese monarchy to look the other way.

The monarchy did look the other way, at least in the early years. The Khampas' forays into Tibet were limited to strikes along the PLA-constructed Lhasa-Xingjian road – a three-day horse ride from Mustang. The number of Tibetan freedom fighters grew, however, and further expanded when warriors' families joined the men in the high country.

Mao was fully aware of America's involvement but was powerless to counteract except by pressuring Nepal's king to oust the rebels from Mustang. The rebels were more than an annoyance to Mao. The *Chushi-Gangdruk* was keeping up a steady flow of ambushes on Chinese convoys which, among other things, provided the US State Department with some of the best intelligence ever received about Mao's People's Liberation Army.

Nevertheless, Nepal's king remained ambivalent throughout the 1960s. He even allowed Tibetan refugee camps to be built south of Mustang in and around the old salt route market town of Pokhara; this was with the help of Washington financing.

It may be argued that the monarch's reluctance to oust the rebels was primarily informed by American aid, which dwarfed other foreign assistance at that time. But it can also be argued that a centuries-old symbiotic relationship between Nepal and Tibet – extensive migration, intermarriage and a partial absorption of Tibetan Buddhism into Nepali Hinduism – created a natural affinity between the two cultures where none existed with their Chinese counterparts. The political problems created by the presence of a refugee population were perhaps offset by the spiritual affinity Nepal shared with Tibet.

The tide was about to turn.

The Khampas' strike-and-run missions were achieving diminishing results. Mao's devastating Cultural Revolution in the mid-1960s broadened China's political and military control in Tibet. The Khampas' goal was and always had been to take back their country. As the decade rolled by, that goal grew further from their reach. Why had they spent the best years of their lives fighting, when they could have acquired civilian skills or started new lives that would have allowed them to support their families? Morale sank among the troops.

Nepal's tacit support of the Khampas was also waning. Chinese pressure on King Mahendra to evict the Khampas from Mustang was nearing the tipping point. The inhabitants of Mustang now resented the Khampas. In the best of times, the agricultural season was brief and could barely support the locals' needs. With the additional strain of the Khampas vying for Mustang crops and forage for livestock, food shortage became a pivotal issue.

And then, in 1972, King Mahendra died. It was the beginning of the end for the Khampas. Prince Birendra, Nepal's heir apparent was far more eager to improve relations with China than his father. Birendra had made a trip to Beijing the previous year and returned to Nepal determined to reap the economic benefits of Chinese patronage.

Even more devastating for the Khampas was President Nixon's 1972 decision to seek rapprochement with China. Henry Kissinger was sent to conduct secret talks with Mao Zedong. Mao made it clear that the CIA would have to discontinue its operation in Nepal before rapprochement could be realized. Almost overnight, Washington cut off its aid to the Mustang resistance. The Khampas were stunned but clung to the hope that at least the Dalai Lama's Government-in-Exile – based in Dharamsala, India – would continue to support Mustang efforts. After all, it had been the *Chushi-Gangdruk* who had ensured the Dalai Lama's safe escape to India in 1959.

In 1973, King Birendra forced the Mustang issue by delivering an ultimatum. Kathmandu diplomatic initiatives were begun with the Khampas' leader, General Wangdu, the gist of which was to either disarm and quit Mustang or be prepared to face the full brunt of the Royal Nepal Army.

Wangdu made a series of trips south to Kathmandu, only to return to his Mustang troops with an ever-bleaker view of reclaiming Tibet. Actually, King Birendra offered the Khampas a generous settlement, particularly in light of Nepal's meager resources: Those who surrendered peacefully would be offered refugee status, interest-free loans, allocation of limited acreage and an education for Khampa children. But the warriors' reluctance to give up the fight – which would be paramount to admitting that they had wasted the best years of their lives on a futile mission – coupled with their distrust of the Nepal government, stymied negotiations.

What finally broke the will of the Khampas was a tape-recorded message from the Dalai Lama. In the spring of 1974, his plea was hand-delivered and played to the thirteen Mustang resistance camps. His message stated that the *Chushi-Gangdruk*'s continuing existence harmed the Government-in-Exile's position vis-à-vis various foreign powers. The time had come to lay down their arms and join their families awaiting them in India and the settlements springing up farther south in Nepal.

In the meantime, nine Royal Nepal Army (RNA) units mobilized from Pokhara, headed up the Kali Gandaki gorge (the deepest in the world, slicing through two of the highest mountains in the world, Annapurna and Dhaulagiri) and converged in Jomsom, the southern-most outpost in Mustang. The RNA spread out, patrolling the area and significantly interrupting communications between Tibetan units and their supporters from the south. The noose was tightening from the north as well: General Wangdu received reports from the Tibetan border that an unspecified number of Chinese troops had broached Mustang soil.

After last-ditch diplomatic efforts failed and the deadline for peaceful disarmament had passed, King Birendra ordered his troops to move in on the camps. The Khampas lay down their arms without letting off a single round. General Wangdu, however, was conspicuously absent. He and eighteen of his loyal subordinates had made a getaway the day before. His objective was to reach India so that he could deliver a satchel of vital intelligence to the CIA's safe house in Delhi.

A high-altitude three-week horse chase ensued, spanning the entire breadth of the western Nepali Himalaya.

September 15, 1974: In a textbook example of military precision, the RNA, which had finally received accurate intelligence about Wangdu's escape route, set up an ambush at Tinker's Pass – one mile from the Indian border. General Wangdu and most of his men were mowed down by the RNA.

Wangdu's bullet-ridden body was airlifted by helicopter to the nation's capital. His corpse was put on display in the central parade grounds of Kathmandu. Thousands of Nepalis lined up to see the body.

Tibetan armed resistance was over.

***

The last of the remaining Mustang freedom fighters traveled south in search of loved ones. Many of their families had settled in refugee camps cropping up in Nepal. They were located in the Kathmandu Valley and, further west, there were five camps established in and around

Chushi-Gangdruk arriving in Pokhara to re-settle with their families

Pokhara: Jampaling, Tashiling, Paljorling, Tashi Palkhiel and Tashi Ghang. Once an important market town along the ancient salt route, Pokhara had become a major tourist destination for Western trekkers and sightseers.

During the formative years of the refugee camps, the Nepali government was quite supportive. The kingdom provided land for the settlers and sanctioned the operation of a Tibetan-run Welfare Office and an Office-of-the-Dalai-Lama, both located in Kathmandu. These organizations proved to be effective systems for dealing with the constant influx of refugees flowing in from Chinese-occupied Tibet. By 2000, the number of refugees entering Nepal averaged 2500 per year.

However, in 2005, under pressure from Beijing, King Gyanendra closed down both Tibetan offices on the grounds that they had not been registered properly – despite operating in an open, transparent manner since the 1960s.

***

Today, Tibetan refugees fall into two categories: Tibetans who arrived in or before 1989 and Tibetans who fled China after 1989.

The first group is allowed to reside in designated regions of Nepal, principally the settlements established in the 1960s and 1970s. Generally speaking, they are treated with tolerance, although no law defines their status. They remain there solely by grace of government policy, which is reinforced by international pressure, chiefly from the United States and the UN Refugee Agency (UNHCR). Resident certificate (RC) cards were made available to the first group, but in the ensuing decades the RCs proved to be of limited value. Of the 20,000 Tibetans living in Nepal today, less than half of the refugees in Nepal have RC cards.

The second group – those who entered Nepal after 1989 – are regarded as illegal aliens by the government. Since 1989, however, by virtue of an informal arrangement with Nepal, UNHCR has been permitted to facilitate the transit of newly arriving Tibetan refugees to continue on to India. There is one caveat: The refugees are on their own until the UNHCR is either notified of their presence in northern Nepal or until the Tibetans can get down to the Tibetan Reception Center in Kathmandu, which serves as a holding pen for new arrivals.

Deportation to China is the exception, not the rule. Nepal generally treats Tibetans on an ad hoc basis, prescribed by the Ministries of Home and Foreign Affairs. The vast majority of the exiles end up in India. But there are also documented cases of Tibetans who, in the last decade, have been deported to China. The fate of those Tibetans is not known but the Chinese regard them as criminals.

As it stands, Tibetans in Nepal are basically without rights, other than to be in Nepal. They are not allowed to own property, register marriages or the births of children. Since 2008, a new penalty for being a Tibetan in Nepal has been introduced: They are no longer permitted to publicly celebrate the birthday of their spiritual leader, the Dalai Lama.

Mikel Dunham
Recent arrivals to Nepal: They fled China with their parents by traversing the Himalaya on foot

Economically, the Tibetan population finds itself hopelessly impoverished. The carpet industry, which in the early years was a booming business, fell out of favor with the European market, signaling the end of a crucial source of income. Today, making trinkets for tourists, receiving small pensions and working negligible farm plots constitute the main sources of income for Tibetans stranded in refugee settlements. None of these offer growth potential. As a result, the younger generation is leaving the camps in ever-larger numbers, in search of jobs and higher education elsewhere. The youth who apply for career-type jobs in Nepal – even if they have attained higher degrees – find it a futile process. Of course, without the requisite RC card, obtaining work or education visas to foreign countries is all the more difficult.

Politically, the refugees have never been as heavily censored as they are at the present time. In 2008, during the months leading up to the Beijing Olympics, Tibetans demonstrated on a daily basis near the

Chinese Embassy in Kathmandu. Their protests made world headlines. This brought into sharp focus the Tibetans' ability to tarnish China's international reputation over human rights. Since the Olympics, therefore, each successive Nepali government has made it clear that anti-China demonstrations will not be tolerated within its borders. Known activists from the settlements are now preemptively arrested prior to political or Dalai Lama-related anniversaries.

The Sino-Tibetan border has also been tightened by security forces on both sides of the frontier – thus making it increasingly dangerous for Tibetans to enter Nepal from the north. If captured along the border, imprisonment in Chinese jails is inevitable.

2008 Anti-Chinese protests in Kathmandu

Except for the very old, (who are too frail to travel or start a new life), most Tibetan exiles would jump at the chance to leave Nepal. Interestingly, during the Bush administration, the U. S. government offered to re-settle Tibetans on American soil. But the offer was rebuffed – presumably under pressure from Beijing – and no successive Nepali government has been willing to reconsider, although the offer is still on the table.

Thus, in spite of their remarkable resilience and abiding faith in Buddhism, Tibetans in Nepal live in a precarious environment of grim restrictions and mounting insecurity created by China's increasing pressure on the Nepali government.

Western tourists may be inspired by the unique sight of Tibetans circumambulating the prayer-flag-festooned stupa of Bodhanath, but the reality is that the Tibetans are – on an equally profound level – illustrating the path, the vicious circle of their temporal entrapment. Tibetans are caught in Nepal. And they see no way out.

Centrality of Buddhism
in the Tibetan
Refugee Community

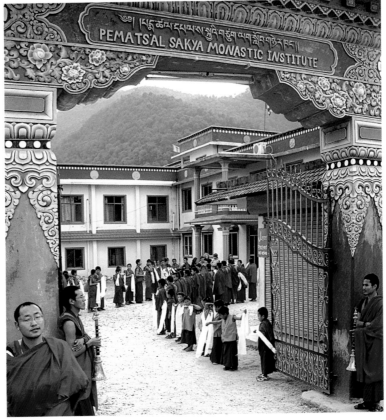

The Dalai Lama's presence in Tibetan temples

Jangchup Choeling Monastery, Tashi Palkhul

Publicly displaying the Dalai Lama's portrait is no longer allowed in Nepal

Monk with his students

Candlelight ceremony, Paljorling

Tashi Shongpa dance, World Peace Day

Nun leaning against a prayer-wheel at Boudhanath

Monk sweeping stairway of Buddha, Kathmandu

Youth in costume for Deity Dance performed in Pokhara

Creating a sand mandala

Public phone: Waiting to speak to relatives in Tibet

Preparing butter lamps for altars

Painting *tormas* (butter sculptures) for altar

Cleaning mani rock, Jangchup Choeling, Tashi Palkhul

Overhead view of monks assembling in temple

Young monks on innoculation day

Speech on the death anniversary of Shakya Pandita Kunga

Giant prayer-wheel, Boudhanath

Meditation break: Practitioners' prayer-wheels in their stands

Stupa of Boudhanath

Selling butter lamps on Buddha's birthday

Early morning *chora*, Boudhanath

Buying pigment as
an offering to keep
Boudhanath's stupa
white

Growing up, Growing Old

Learning the English ABCs

Nursery school, Pokhara

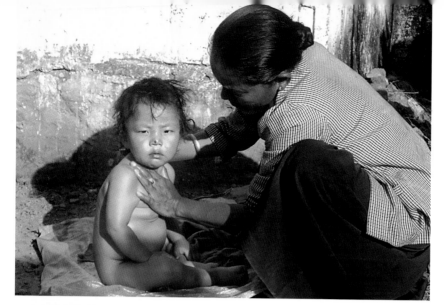

A priority for parents is the best possible education for their children, with an emphasis on learning English. Foreign donors have helped considerably in this regard. But in the smaller settlements, even the price of pencils and writing paper can be a challenge for families. Higher education is a far greater challenge.

Here, we see parents strapping a banner to the bus that will take younger students on an Educational Tour. It is an important day for the community.

Dancing after a wedding

Outing at Phewa Lake, Pokhara

Hanging out at a Pokhara pool hall

Working in a tourist shop, Thamel distict, Kathmandu

Video game

Card game played on "Nine Bad Omens Day"

Sho-pa-ra played on "Nine Bad Omens Day"

Board game played on "Nine Bad Omens Day"

Pouring hot butter tea from churn

Cooking in the communal kitchen

Vegetable garden

Corn field

Making *khabtse*

Preparing potatoes for communal kitchen

Drying noodles

De-sil, rice prepared with dried fruit, and the traditional butter tea

Tikmo (dumplings) ready to be cooked

Washing dishes

Feeding pigeons and talking on a cell phone

Youth clipping grandmother's fingernails

Buddhist crematory, Ramghat

Pouring tea for old man

Old People's Home

Spinning prayer-wheels at Old People's Home

View of Himalaya from Pokhara settlement

Prayerflags, ground level

Phewa Lake, setting for the tourist town of Pokhara

Tibetan side-street in Pokhara

Entrance to Pokhara refugee settlement in Pokhara

Far less well known are the four refugee camps outside of Pokhara.
Above is the main road to Tashi Palkhiel.

To the upper right is a refugee school in the hinterlands.

Lower right: The thatched-roof construction is an example of refugee
homes, originally regarded as temporary housing. Now, after many
decades, these homes are seen as permanent domiciles. Today,
few Tibetans stranded in Nepal hope to be able to return to their
motherland.

Monk looking at the Tibetan goods offered for tourists

Spinning wool for carpets for the tourist trade

Tending to the sheep

Rest spot by the wall of the monastery

Preparing the string for a carpet

Tamping down the wool

Final trimming of
finished carpet

First thing in the morning: waiting for tourists in Pokhara

The strength of the Tibetan refugee population in Nepal resides in their deep sense of community.

Above: The Camp Management Committee

Upper right: Community members making *kaptse* for holiday celebrations

Lower right: One of Tibetan's favorite pastimes, a picnic

Moving old community kitchen by hand

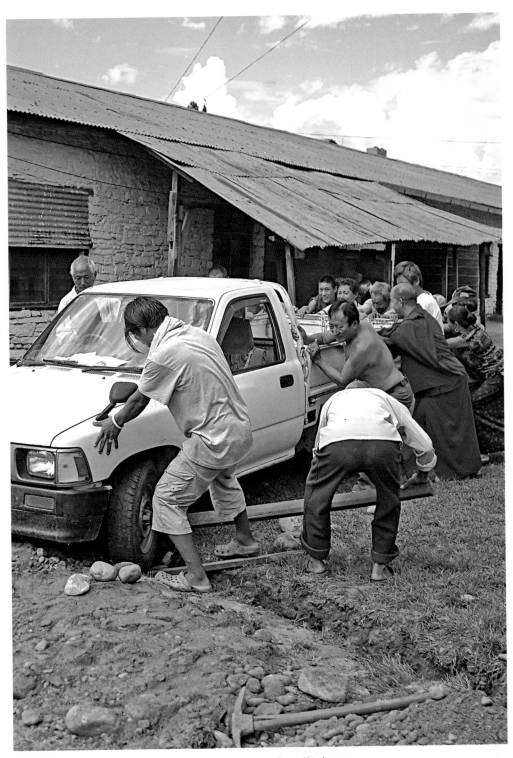

Monks joining forces to get truck out of a ditch

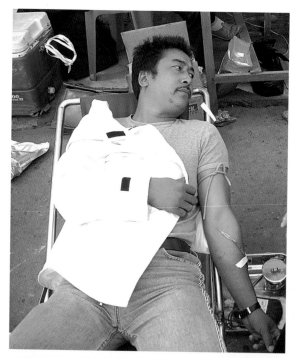

Tibetan donating blood in Pokhara

Selling a Tibetan newspaper in Kathmandu

Helping with the babies

Community secretary addresses New Year's cards to sponsors and
friends of the settlement

Re-painting basketball court

Moving firewood

Re-painting monastery exterior

Stitching sheep skin for a mattress

Traditional thankas painters

Applique thanka maker

Tibetan tailor making *chuba*

Saving on gas

A new shop at the settlement

Traditional Tibetan pharmacy comprised of herbal medicines

Regional bus stop

Pilgrimage to holy places is an important aspect of Buddhist practice.

Here, refugees have been bussed to Sarnath, India, where the historical Buddha gave his first sermon: "The Four Noble Truths." The Mahabodhi Temple, which houses relics of the Buddha, can be seen in the lower right.

Sarnath, India: The Dhamek Stupa was built in 249 BCE to commemorate Buddha's first sermon, given to his five disciples, which revealed the "Eightfold Noble Path Leading to Enlightenment."

Observing
Non-Tibetans

Nepali woman atop Tibetan mani boulder

Nepali vendor of Tibetan *malas* (roseries)

Tibetan audience watching a Japanese monk bowing to Boudhanath
Stupa

Nepali women making offerings at Boudhanath

Nepalis doing *chora* around Boudhanath stupa

Nepali fruit seller

Phoning the police: Nepali restaurant owner holds back two customers who tried to skip their bill

Nepali vegetable market in Pokhara

Nepali beggar

Nighttime demonstration: Maoists in Pokhara

Daytime demonstration: Nepali Congress protesters, Pokhara

Nepali money changer writing daily rates

Gurang band performing at a Pokhara street festival

Political Struggle

Community youths produce a play for the settlement. A BBC reporter interviews a Tibetan monk (in Tibet). Chinese authorities arrest, then torture, then kill the monastic human rights dissidents for talking to the international press.

Tibetan protesters in Kathmandu

Monks on a farm vehicle

Police response to Tibetan protests in Boudhanath

Sentiment painted on wall at a basketball court

Acknowledgements

On every level, *Caught in Nepal* has been a collaborative project. Apart from the fine work achieved by the amateur Tibetan photographers, there has been overwhelming international support.

First and foremost, thanks must be given to the William Hinman Foundation, which has supported this book from the very beginning.

To my Nepali posse, who have accompanied me through the hinterlands and stuck their necks out for me – Govinda Rijal, Deepak Bhujel, Bishnu Simkhada and Kapil Shrestha – thanks for the wild rides and time-proven loyalty.

As always, Lisa Choegyal receives a standing ovation.

To Mary Beth Markey and Kate Saunders, thanks for many years of wit, hard facts and support shared precisely when it is most needed.

A salute to Simeon Schnapper and Joe Scarpa – the former for his computerized magic carpet, the latter for his invisible fund-driving bulldozer.

In the final stage of the book's production, which required one final and crucial financial boost, I launched a pledge drive on kickstarter.com. The results were fantastic due, in part, to the very generous donations from the following patrons:

Jack Owens, Laura Haas, Natalie La Padura, Jason La Padura, David Morin, Melanie Wyler, Matthew and Tina Miller, Romanos Isaac, Joe Rath, Andrew Reznik, Daniella Hirschfeld, Jacquelin Leary, Vicki Mortimer, Cynthia Norman, Robert Baker, Ruth McMahon, David Holland, Chris Carelli, Linda Wilson, David Manning, Edna De Jesus, Melissa Atkinson, Elizabeth and Karma Gongde, Larry and Sandra Sims, Fiona Chadwick, Scott Goddard and Gautum SJB Rana.

Finally there are four benefactors, who deserve separate pages of recognition. My Tibetan colleagues and I will always be grateful to you.

118

Guido Freddi and Ilaria Borrelli

Michael Azeez

Trudi Butler Howley

The International Campaign for Tibet works to promote human rights and democratic freedoms for the Tibetan people. Whether advocating for fundamental freedoms, working with governments to press for an open and progressive political system in the People's Republic of China, or mobilizing supporters around the world, ICT is mindful that our work must be led by priorities on the ground.

For new Tibetan refugees, the experience of oppression and the elation of freedom can be less immediately vital in their dangerous crossing through the high Himalayas than finding food or keeping warm. Thanks to support garnered in the international community, these emergency needs can be met. But for long-staying Tibetan refugees in Nepal and India, constraints on their ambitions due to the their lack of citizen status can create obstacles in their onward journey. ICT continues to challenge limitations imposed on long-staying Tibetan refugees and, with the Central Tibetan Administration of His Holiness the Dalai Lama, looks for opportunities to foster sustainability in these exile communities.

To be involved in the work of the International Campaign for Tibet on behalf of Tibetans in and out of Tibet, please visit

www.savetibet.org

The International Campaign for Tibet is a duly registered not-for-profit organization with offices in Washington, D.C., Amsterdam, Brussels and Berlin, field offices in Kathmandu and Dharamsala, and capacities in London and Geneva.

INTERNATIONAL
CAMPAIGN
FOR TIBET